1935...
read a go...
either a lot of...
Cheap paperbac... ...ut their
poor production generally mirrored the quality
between the covers. One weekend that year,
Allen Lane, Managing Director of The Bodley Head,
having spent the weekend visiting Agatha Christie,
found himself on a platform at Exeter station trying to
find something to read for his journey back to London.
He was appalled by the quality of the material he had to
choose from. Everything that Allen Lane achieved from that
day until his death in 1970 was based on a passionate belief
in the existence of 'a vast reading public for *intelligent*
books at a low price'. The result of his momentous vision
was the birth not only of Penguin, but of the 'paperback
revolution'. Quality writing became available for the price of
a packet of cigarettes, literature became a mass medium
for the first time, a nation of book-borrowers became a
nation of book-buyers – and the very concept of book
publishing was changed for ever. Those founding
principles – of quality and value, with an overarching
belief in the fundamental importance of reading –
have guided everything the company has
done since 1935. Sir Allen Lane's
pioneering spirit is still very much alive
at Penguin in 2005. Here's to
the next 70 years!

MORE THAN A BUSINESS

'We decided it was time to end the almost customary half-hearted manner in which cheap editions were produced – as though the only people who could possibly want cheap editions must belong to a lower order of intelligence. We, however, believed in the existence in this country of a vast reading public for intelligent books at a low price, and staked everything on it'
Sir Allen Lane, 1902–1970

'The Penguin Books are splendid value for sixpence, so splendid that if other publishers had any sense they would combine against them and suppress them'
George Orwell

'More than a business … a national cultural asset'
Guardian

'When you look at the whole Penguin achievement you know that it constitutes, in action, one of the more democratic successes of our recent social history'
Richard Hoggart

On Seeing and Noticing

ALAIN DE BOTTON

PENGUIN BOOKS

PENGUIN BOOKS

Published by the Penguin Group
Penguin Books Ltd, 80 Strand, London WC2R ORL, England
Penguin Group (USA) Inc., 375 Hudson Street, New York, New York 10014, USA
Penguin Group (Canada), 10 Alcorn Avenue, Toronto, Ontario, Canada M4V 3B2
(a division of Pearson Penguin Canada Inc.)
Penguin Ireland, 25 St Stephen's Green, Dublin 2, Ireland
(a division of Penguin Books Ltd)
Penguin Group (Australia), 250 Camberwell Road, Camberwell, Victoria 3124,
Australia (a division of Pearson Australia Group Pty Ltd)
Penguin Books India Pvt Ltd, 11 Community Centre,
Panchsheel Park, New Delhi – 110 017, India
Penguin Group (NZ), cnr Airborne and Rosedale Roads, Albany,
Auckland 1310, New Zealand (a division of Pearson New Zealand Ltd)
Penguin Books (South Africa) (Pty) Ltd, 24 Sturdee Avenue,
Rosebank 2196, South Africa

Penguin Books Ltd, Registered Offices: 80 Strand, London WC2R ORL, England

www.penguin.com

First published as a Pocket Penguin 2005

1

Copyright © Alain de Botton, 2005
All rights reserved

The moral right of the author has been asserted

The publisher is grateful to Picador for permission
to reprint 'On Authenticity' from *Essays in Love*

Set in 10.5/12.5pt Monotype Dante
Typeset by Palimpsest Book Production Limited
Polmont, Stirlingshire
Printed in England by Clays Ltd, St Ives plc

Contents

On the Pleasures of Sadness

Edward Hopper belongs to that category of artists whose work is sad but does not make us sad – the painterly counterpart to Bach or Leonard Cohen. Loneliness is the dominant theme in his art. His figures look as though they are far from home, they stand reading a letter on the edge of a hotel bed or drinking in a bar, they gaze out of the window of a moving train or read a book in a hotel lobby. Their faces are vulnerable and introspective. They have perhaps just left someone or been left, they are in search of work, sex or company, adrift in transient places. It is often night and through the window lie the darkness and threat of the open country or of a strange city. And yet despite the bleakness Hopper's paintings depict, they are not themselves bleak to look at – perhaps because they allow viewers to witness an echo of their own griefs and disappointments, and thereby to feel less personally persecuted and beset by them. It is perhaps sad books that console us most when we are sad, and the pictures of lonely service stations that we should hang on our walls when there is no one to hold or love.

In *Automat* (1927), a woman sits alone drinking a cup of coffee. It is late and, to judge by her hat and coat, cold outside. The room seems large, brightly lit and empty. The décor is functional, with a stone-topped table, hard-wearing black wooden chairs and white walls. The woman looks self-conscious and slightly afraid, unused to sitting alone in a public place. Something appears to have gone wrong. She unwittingly invites the viewer to imagine stories for her, stories of betrayal or loss. She is trying not to let her hand shake as she moves the coffee cup to her lips. It may be eleven at night in February in a large North American city.

Automat is a picture of sadness – and yet it is not a sad picture. It has the power of a great melancholy piece of music. Despite the starkness of the furnishings, the location itself does not seem wretched. Others in the room may be on their own, men and women drinking coffee by themselves, similarly lost in thought, similarly distanced from society: a common isolation with the beneficial effect of lessening the oppressive sense within any one person that they are alone in being alone. Hopper invites us to feel empathy with the woman in her isolation. She seems dignified and generous, only perhaps a little too trusting, a little naïve – as if she has knocked against a hard corner of the world. Hopper puts us on her side, the side of the outsider against the insiders.

In roadside diners and late-night cafeterias, hotel lobbies and station cafés, we too may dilute a feeling of isolation in a lonely public place and hence rediscover a distinctive sense of community. The lack of domesticity, the bright lights and anonymous furniture may be a relief from what can be the false comforts of home. It may be easier to give way to sadness here than in a living room with wallpaper and framed photos, the décor of a refuge that has let us down. The figures in Hopper's art are not opponents of home per se, it is simply that, in a variety of undefined ways, home appears to have betrayed them, forcing them out into the night or on to the road. The twenty-four-hour diner, the station waiting room or motel are sanctuaries for those who have, for noble reasons, failed to find a home in the ordinary world.

A side effect of coming into contact with any great artist

is that we start to notice things in the world that we can understand, thanks to the work, that the painter would have been receptive to. We become sensitized to what one might call the Hopperesque, a quality now found not only in the North American locales where Hopper himself went, but also anywhere in the developed world where there are motels and service stations, roadside diners and airports, bus stations and all-night supermarkets. Hopper is the father of a whole school of art which finds as its subject matter 'liminal' spaces, buildings that lie outside homes and offices, places of transit where we are aware of a particular kind of alienated poetry. We feel Hopper's presence behind the photographs of Andreas Gursky and Hannah Starkey, the films of Wim Wenders and the books of Thomas Bernhardt.

I remember finding the Hopperesque one evening in a service station off the motorway between London and Manchester. Objectively speaking, it wasn't a beautiful building. The lighting was unforgiving, bringing out pallor and blemishes. The chairs and seats, painted in childishly bright colours, had the strained jollity of a fake smile. No one in the station was talking, no one admitting to curiosity or fellow feeling. We gazed blankly past one another at the serving counter or out into the darkness. We might have been seated among rocks. I sat in one corner, eating fingers of chocolate and taking occasional sips of orange juice. I felt lonely but, for once, this was a gentle, even pleasant kind of loneliness because, rather than unfolding against a backdrop of laughter and fellowship, in which I would suffer from a contrast between my mood and the environment, this loneliness unfolded in a place where everyone was a stranger, where the difficulties of communication and the frustrated longing for love seemed to be acknowledged and brutally celebrated by the architecture and lighting.

Service stations always evoke for me Hopper's *Gas*, painted thirteen years before *Automat* and, like the earlier picture, also a study of isolation. We see a petrol station standing on its own in the impending darkness. But in Hopper's hands, the isolation is again made poignant and enticing. The darkness that spreads like a fog from the right of the canvas, a harbinger of fear, contrasts with the security of the station. Against the backdrop of night and wild woods, in this last outpost of humanity, a sense of kinship may be easier to develop than in daylight in the city. The coffee machine and magazines, tokens of small human desires and vanities, stand in opposition to the wide non-human world outside, to the miles of forest in which branches crack occasionally under the footfall of bears and foxes. There is something touching in the suggestion – made in bold pink on the cover of one magazine – that we paint our nails purple this summer and an invocation above the coffee machine that we sample the aroma of freshly roasted beans. In this last stop before the road enters the endless forest, what we have in common with others can loom larger than what separates us.

It's a curious feature of Hopper's work that though it seems concerned to show us places that are transient and unhomely, we may, in contact with it, feel as if we have been carried back to some important place in ourselves, a place of stillness and sadness, of seriousness and authenticity: it can help us to remember ourselves. How is it possible to forget 'oneself'? At stake is not a literal forgetting of practical data, rather a forgetting of those parts of ourselves with which a particular sense of integrity and well-being appears to be bound up. We have many different selves, not all of which feel equally like 'us', a division we confront most clearly in relation to our physical appearance, where we may judge that the person a photographer has captured, while something to do with the being bearing our name, in fact has very little connection with the spirit and attitude we would choose to identify with. This visual dynamic has a psychological equivalent, for within our own minds too, we are made aware of constellations of ideas and moods distinct enough to feel like different personalities – an inner fluidity which can on occasion lead us to declare, without any allusion to the supernatural, that we are not feeling as if we are ourselves.

On looking at a picture, we may recognize it as being at once important to us, but out of our ordinary reach – and one of the things we may be trying to do in buying the postcard of it and hanging it prominently above the desk (as I have done with a number of Hopper's works) is to have it as an omnipresent, solid token of the emotional texture of the person we want to be and feel we deep down are. By seeing the picture every day, the hope is that a little of its qualities will rub off on us. What we may welcome in the picture isn't so much the subject matter as the tone, it is the record of an emotional attitude conveyed through colour and form. We know we will of course drift far from it, that it won't be possible or even practical to hold on to the picture's mood for ever, and that we will have to be many different people (with bold opinions and a sense of certainty, with casual wit and parental authority), but we welcome it as a reminder and an anchor.

Hopper also took an interest in cars and trains. He was drawn to the introspective mood that travelling seems to put us into. He was interested in capturing the atmosphere inside half-empty carriages making their way across a landscape: the silence that reigns inside while the wheels beat in rhythm against the rails outside, the dreaminess fostered by the noise and the view from the windows, a dreaminess in which we seem to stand outside our normal selves and have access to thoughts and memories that may not emerge in more settled circumstances. The woman in Hopper's *Compartment C, Car 293* (1938) seems in such a frame of mind, reading her book and shifting her gaze between the carriage and the view.

Few places are more conducive to internal conversations than a moving plane, ship or train. There is an almost quaint correlation between what is in front of our eyes and the thoughts we are able to have in our heads: large thoughts at times requiring large views, new thoughts new places. Introspective reflections which are liable to stall are helped along by the flow of the landscape. The mind may be reluctant to think properly when thinking is all it is supposed to do. The task can be as paralysing as having to tell a joke or mimic an accent on demand. Thinking improves when parts of the mind are given other tasks, are charged with listening to music or following a line of trees. The music or the view distracts for a time that nervous, censorious, practical part of the mind which is inclined to shut down when it notices something difficult emerging in consciousness and which runs scared of memories, longings, introspective or original ideas and prefers instead the administrative and the impersonal.

Of all modes of transport, the train is perhaps the best aid to thought: the views have none of the potential monotony of those on a ship or plane, they move fast enough for us not to get exasperated but slowly enough to allow us to identify objects. They offer us brief, inspiring glimpses into private domains, letting us see a woman at the moment when she takes a cup from a shelf in her kitchen, before carrying us on to a patio where a man is sleeping and then to a park where a child is catching a ball thrown by a figure we cannot see.

At the end of hours of train-dreaming, we may feel we have been returned to ourselves: that is, brought back into contact with emotions and ideas of importance to us. It is not necessarily at home that we best encounter our true selves. The furniture insists that we cannot change because it does not; the domestic setting keeps us tethered to the person we are in ordinary life, but who may not be who we essentially are.

Hotels offer a similar opportunity to escape our habits of mind and it is unsurprising that Hopper painted them repeatedly (*Hotel Room*, 1931, *Hotel Lobby*, 1943, *Rooms for Tourists*, 1945, *Hotel by a Railroad*, 1952, *Hotel Window*, 1956 and *Western Motel*, 1957). Lying in bed in a hotel, the room quiet except for the occasional swooshing of an elevator in the innards of the building, we can draw a line under what preceded our arrival, we can overfly great and ignored stretches of our experience. We can reflect upon our lives from a height we could not have reached in the midst of everyday business – subtly assisted in this by the unfamiliar world around us: by the small wrapped soaps on the edge of the basin, by the gallery of miniature bottles in the minibar, by the room-service menu with its promises of all-night dining and the view on to an unknown city stirring silently twenty-five floors below us. Hotel notepads can be the recipients of unexpectedly intense, revelatory thoughts, taken down in the early hours.

If a feature of love is an overcoming of loneliness, it is only fitting that, a few weeks after we met, my now-wife and I realized that we shared a love of alienated Hopperesque spaces and, in particular, of Little Chef restaurants. Little Chefs are to British life what the diner is to America: ugly places full of bad food that are nevertheless resonant with poetry. My wife had been taken to Little Chefs as a little girl by her father, a man of few words who liked to order an English breakfast, read the paper and gaze out of the window smoking a cigarette, saying nothing. It had felt like a break from routine, from the monotony of growing up in a dull Suffolk market town. The menu was bright, someone brought the food to your table and there might be a slide to play on outside. She had always gone for the Jubilee pancakes and once on her birthday had had two orders and been sick over the back of the family car. Then, at university, Little Chefs had been a place to go to when she wanted to get away from the hothouse atmosphere of her campus and see more ordinary life roll by for a while.

For my part, I remembered going to Little Chefs with my parents as a rare treat – or funerary rite – before returning to boarding school. It was a symbol of a multi-coloured, warm cheerful world that I wanted to hang on to for ever, so vivid was its contrast with the place I was headed for. Then, grown up, in a long and painfully lonely period in my mid twenties, I'd SOMETIMESdrive out of London to have a solitary lunch in a Little Chef. It felt comforting to drown my own alienation in a wholeheartedly alienated environment. It felt like reading Schopenhauer when one is down. Little Chefs are in many ways about loneliness; about a particularly English kind of loneliness even. They both represent and are a curious cure for it.

Thanks to the unlikely setting of a Little Chef, we can for a time escape some of the constraints of home, of our habits of mind, of the rules of sophisticated society – and enjoy a beguiling vision of an alternative life. To identify a common taste in Little Chefs doesn't just mean sharing a taste in restaurants, it means sharing a piece of inner, very private psychology. It's a wonder they don't hold more wedding parties there.

Oscar Wilde once remarked that there had been no fog in London before Whistler had painted it. There was of course lots of fog, it was just that little bit harder to notice its qualities without the example of Whistler to direct our gaze. What Wilde said of Whistler, we may well say of Hopper: that there were far fewer service stations, Little Chefs, airports, trains, motels and diners visible in the world before Edward Hopper began painting.

On Going to the Airport

When we're feeling sad and bored at home, one of the better places to head to is the airport. Not in order to fly – there's no quicker way to hate an airport than to have to use it, but, rather, to admire it, as one might a picture or, perhaps more accurately, a ballet.

On a grey day, from the edge of the runway at Heathrow, a 747 appears at first as a small brilliant white light, a star dropping towards earth. It has been in the air for some twelve hours. It took off from Bangkok at dawn. It flew over the Bay of Bengal, Delhi, the Afghan desert and the Caspian Sea. It traced a course over Romania, the Czech Republic and began its descent, so gently that few passengers would have noticed a change of tone in the engines, above the coast of Normandy. From the ground, the white light gradually takes shape as a vast two-storied body with four engines suspended like earrings beneath implausibly long wings. In the light rain, clouds of water form a veil behind the plane on its matronly progress towards the airfield. The plane is a symbol of worldliness, carrying within itself a trace of all the lands it has crossed; its eternal mobility offering an imaginative counterweight to feelings of stagnation and confinement. This morning the plane was over the Malay Peninsula, a phrase in which there lingers the smells of guava and sandalwood. And now, a few metres above the earth which it has avoided for so long, the plane appears motionless, its nose raised upwards, seeming to pause before its sixteen rear wheels meet the tarmac with a blast of smoke that makes manifest its speed and weight.

On a parallel runway, an A340 ascends for New York and retracts its flaps and wheels, which it won't require again until the descent over the white clapboard houses of Long Beach, 3,000 miles and eight hours of sea-and-cloud away. Visible through the heat haze of turbofans, other planes wait to start their journeys. All across the airfield, planes are on the move, their fins a confusion of colours against the grey horizon, like sails at a regatta.

Along the glass-and-steel back of the terminal rest three giants, whose liveries indicate a varied provenance: Canada, Pakistan, Korea. For a few hours, their wing-tips will lie only a few metres apart, before each set begins another journey into the stratospheric winds. As every ship turns into a gate, a choreographed dance begins. Trucks slip to the underbelly, black fuel hoses are fastened to the wings, a gangway bends its rectangular rubber lips over the fuselage. The doors of the holds are opened to withdraw battered aluminium cargo crates, perhaps containing fruit that only a few days ago hung from the branches of tropical trees or vegetables that had their roots in the soil of high silent valleys. Two men in overalls set up a small ladder next to one engine and open up its casing to reveal an intricate terrain of wires and small steel pipes. Sheets and pillows are lowered from the front of one cabin. Passengers disembark for whom this ordinary afternoon will have a supernatural tinge.

Nowhere is the appeal of the airport more concentrated than in the television screens which hang in rows from terminal ceilings announcing the departure and arrival of flights and whose absence of aesthetic self-consciousness, whose workmanlike casing and pedestrian typefaces do nothing to disguise their emotional charge nor imaginative appeal. Tokyo, Amsterdam, Istanbul. Warsaw, Singapore, Rio. The screens bear all the poetic resonance of the last line of James Joyce's *Ulysses*: at once a record of where the novel was written and, no less importantly, a symbol of the cosmopolitan spirit behind its composition: 'Trieste, Zurich, Paris.' The constant calls of the screens, some accompanied by the impatient pulsing of a cursor, suggest with what ease our seemingly entrenched lives might be altered, were we to walk down a corridor and on to a craft that in a few hours would land us in a place of which we had no memories and where no one knew our names. How pleasant to hold in mind, through the crevasses of our moods, at three in the afternoon when lassitude and despair threaten, that there is always a plane taking off for somewhere.

Seeing a plane parked at a gate, dwarfing luggage carts and mechanics, one is induced to feel surprise, overriding any scientific explanation, at how such a thing might move – a few metres, let alone to Japan. Buildings, among the few man-made structures of comparable size, do not prepare us for a plane's agility or self-possession; for these buildings are cracked by slight movements of the earth, they leak air and water and lose parts of themselves to the wind.

Few seconds in life are more releasing than those in which a plane ascends to the sky. Looking out of a window from a machine standing stationary at the beginning of a runway, we face a vista of familiar proportions: a road, oil cylinders, grass and hotels with copper-tinted windows; the earth as we have always known it, where we make slow progress, even with the help of a car, where calf muscles and engines strain to reach the summit of hills, where, half a mile ahead or less, there is almost always a line of trees or buildings to restrict our view. Then suddenly, accompanied by the controlled rage of the engines (with only a slight tremor from glasses in the galley), we rise fluently into the atmosphere and an immense horizon opens up across which we can wander without impediment. A journey which on earth would have taken an afternoon can be accomplished with an infinitesimal movement of the eye.

There is psychological pleasure in this take-off too, for the swiftness of the plane's ascent is an exemplary symbol of transformation. The display of power can inspire us to imagine analagous, decisive shifts in our own lives; to imagine that we too might one day surge above much that had loomed over us.

The new vantage point lends order and logic to the landscape: roads curve to avoid hills, rivers trace paths to lakes, pylons lead from power stations to towns, streets that from earth seemed laid out without thought, emerge as well-planned grids. The eye attempts to match what it can see with what it knows should be there, like trying to decipher a familiar book in a new language. And to think that all along, hidden from our sight, our lives were this small: the world we live in but almost never see; the way we must appear to the hawk and to the gods.

The engines show none of the effort required to take us to this place. They hang in the inconceivable cold, patiently and invisibly powering the craft, their sole requests, painted on their inner flanks in red letters, that we do not walk on them and that we feed them 'Oil only: D50TFI-S4', a message for a forthcoming set of men in overalls, 4,000 miles away and still asleep.

There is not much talk about the clouds visible up here. No one thinks it remarkable that somewhere above an ocean we flew past a vast white candy-floss island which would have made a perfect seat for an angel or even God himself in a painting by Piero della Francesca. In the cabin, no one stands up to announce with requisite emphasis that, out of the window, *we are flying over a cloud*, a matter that would have detained Leonardo and Poussin, Claude and Constable.

Food that, if eaten in a kitchen, would have been banal or offensive, acquires a new taste and interest in the presence of the clouds (like a picnic of bread and cheese that delights us when eaten on a clifftop above a pounding sea). With the in-flight tray, we make ourselves at home in this unhomely place: we appropriate the extraterrestrial landscape with the help of a chilled bread roll and a plastic tray of potato salad.

Our airborne companions outside the window look unexpected when scrutinized. In paintings and from the ground, they appear like horizontal ovaloids, but here they resemble giant obelisks made of piles of unsteady shaving foam. Their kinship with steam is clearer, they are more volatile, the product of something that may have just exploded and is still mutating. It remains perplexing that it would be impossible to sit on one.

The clouds usher in tranquillity. Below us are enemies and colleagues, the sites of our terrors and our griefs; all of them now infinitesimal, scratches on the earth. We may know this old lesson in perspective well enough, but rarely does it seem as true as when we are pressed against the cold plane window, our craft a teacher of profound philosophy.

On Authenticity

1. It is one of the ironies of love that it is easiest to confidently seduce those we are least attracted to, an intensity of desire interfering with the requisite indifference, attraction eliciting a sense of inferiority compared with the perfection that we have located in the beloved. My love for Chloe meant I had lost all belief in my own worthiness. Who could *I* be next to *her*? Was it not the greatest honour for her to have agreed to this dinner, to have dressed so elegantly ['*Is this all right?*' she'd asked in the car. '*It had better be, because I'm not changing a sixth time*'], let alone that she be willing to respond to some of the things that might fall [if ever I recovered my tongue] from my unworthy lips?

2. It was Friday night and Chloe and I were seated at a corner table of *Les Liaisons Dangereuses*, a French restaurant that had recently opened at the end of the Fulham Road. There could have been no more appropriate setting for Chloe's beauty, the chandeliers throwing soft shadows across her face, the light green walls matching her light green eyes. And yet, as though struck dumb by the angel that faced me across the table, I found [only minutes after an animated conversation] that I had lost all capacity either to think or speak, able only to silently draw invisible patterns on the starched white table-cloth and take unnecessary sips of bubbled water from a large glass goblet.

3. Out of this perceived inferiority emerged the need to take on a personality that was not directly my own, a seducing self that would locate and respond to the demands of this superior being. Did love condemn me not to be myself? Perhaps not for ever, but, if it was to be taken seriously, it did at this stage of seduction, for the seducing position was one which led me to ask *What would appeal to her?* rather than *What appeals to me?* I asked *How would **she** perceive my tie?* rather than *How do **I** judge it?* Love forced me to look at myself as through the imagined eyes of the beloved. *Not who am I, but who am I for her?* And in the reflexive movement of that question, my self could not help but grow tinged with a certain bad faith and inauthenticity.

4. This inauthenticity did not necessarily manifest itself in flagrant lies or exaggerations. It simply involved trying to anticipate everything Chloe might want, so that I could take on the accent the part demanded.

'Would you like some wine?' I asked her.

'I don't know, would you like wine?' she asked back.

'I really don't mind, if you feel like it,' I replied.

'It's as you please, whatever you want,' she continued.

'Either way is fine with me.'

'I agree.'

'So should we have it or not?'

'Well, I don't think *I'll* have any,' ventured Chloe.

'You're right, I don't feel like any either,' I concurred.

'Let's not have wine then,' she concluded.

'Great, so we'll just stick with the water.'

5. Though authentic selfhood has as its prerequisite the ability to achieve a stable identity irrespective of company, the evening had developed into an inauthentic attempt to locate and shape myself according to Chloe's desires. What did she expect from a man? What were the tastes and orientations according to which I should adjust my behaviour? If staying true to oneself is deemed an essential criterion of moral self-hood, then seduction had led me to resolutely fail the ethical test. Why had I lied about my feelings towards a delicious-looking selection of wines, prominently advertised on a blackboard above Chloe's head? Because my choice had suddenly seemed inadequate and crude next to her mineral thirst. Seduction had split me into two, into a true [alcoholic] self, and a false [aquatic] one.

6. The first course arrived, arranged on plates with the symmetry of a formal French garden.

'It looks too beautiful to touch,' said Chloe [how I knew the feeling], 'I've never eaten grilled tuna like this before.'

We began to eat, but the only sound was that of cutlery against china. There seemed to be nothing to say: Chloe had been my only thought for too long, but the one thought that at this moment I could not share. Silence was a damning indictment. A silence with an unattractive person implies they are the boring one. A silence with an attractive one leaves you certain it is *you* who are impossibly dull.

7. Silence and clumsiness could perhaps be forgiven as rather pitiful proof of desire. It being easy enough to seduce some-one towards whom one feels indifferent, the clumsiest sedu-cers could generously be deemed the most genuine. Not to find the right words may ironically be proof that the right words are meant [if only they could be said]. When, in that other *Liaisons*, the Marquise de Merteuil writes to the

Vicomte de Valmont, she faults him on the fact that his love letters are too perfect, too logical to be the words of a true lover, whose thoughts will be disjointed and for whom the fine phrase will always elude. Language trips up on love, desire lacks articulacy [but how willingly I would at that moment have swapped my constipation for the Vicomte's vocabulary].

8. Given my wish to seduce Chloe, it was essential that I find out more about her. How could I abandon my true self unless I knew what false self to adopt? But this was no easy task, a reminder that understanding another requires hours of careful attention and interpretion, teasing a coherent character from a thousand words and actions. Unfortunately, the patience and intelligence required went far beyond the capacities of my anxious, infatuated mind. I behaved like a reductive social psychologist, eager to press a person into simple definitions, unwilling to apply the care of a novelist to capturing the polyvalence of human nature. Over the first course, I blundered with heavy-handed, interview-like questions: What do you like to read? ['*Joyce, Henry James, Cosmo if there's time*'], Do you like your job? ['*All jobs are pretty crap, don't you think?*'], What country would you live in if you could live anywhere? ['*I'm fine here, anywhere where I don't have to change the plug for my hairdrier*'], What do you like to do on weekends? ['*Go to the movies on Saturday, on Sunday, stock up on chocolate for getting depressed with in the evening.*']

9. Behind such clumsy questions [with every one I asked, I seemed to get further from knowing her], there was an impatient attempt to get to the most direct question of all, '*Who*

are you?' [and hence *'Who should I be?'*]. But such a direct approach was naturally doomed to failure, and the more bluntly I pursued it, the more my subject escaped through the net, letting me know what newspaper she read and music she liked, but not thereby enlightening me as to 'who' she was – a reminder, if ever one needed it, of the 'I''s capacity to elude itself.

10. Chloe hated talking about herself. Perhaps her most obvious feature was a certain modesty and self-deprecation. Whenever the conversation led her to talk on the subject, Chloe did so in the harshest terms. It would not simply be 'I' or 'Chloe', but *'a basket-case like me'* or *'the winner of the Ophelia award for quiet nerves'*. Her self-deprecation was all the more attractive for it seemed free of the veiled appeals of self-pitying people, the double-take self-deprecation of the *I'm so stupid/No, you're not* variety.

11. Her childhood had not been pleasant, but she was stoic about the matter [*'I hate childhood dramatizations that make Job look like he got off lightly'*]. She had been born into a financially comfortable home. Her father [*'All his problems started when his parents called him Barry'*] had been an academic, a professor of law, her mother [*'Claire'*] had for a time run a flower shop. Chloe was the middle child, a girl sandwiched between two favoured and faultless boys. When her older brother died of leukaemia shortly after her eighth birthday, her parents' grief expressed itself as anger at their daughter who, slow at school and sulky around the house, had obstinately clung to life instead of their darling son. She grew up guilty, filled with a sense of blame for what had happened, feelings that her mother did little to alleviate. She liked to pick on a person's

weakest characteristics and not let go – so Chloe was for ever reminded of how badly she performed at school compared to the dead brother, of how gauche she was, and of how disreputable her friends were [criticisms that were not particularly true, but that grew more so with every mention]. Chloe had turned to her father for affection, but the man was as closed with his emotions as he was open with his legal knowledge, which he would pedantically share with her as a substitute, till adolescence when Chloe's frustration with him turned to anger and she openly defied him and everything he stood for [it was fortunate that I had not chosen the legal profession].

12. Of past boyfriends, only hints emerged over the meal: one had worked as a motorcycle mechanic in Italy and had treated her very badly, another, who she had mothered, had ended up in jail for possession of drugs, one had been an analytical philosopher at London University ['*You don't have to be Freud to see he was the daddy I never went to bed with*'], another a test-car driver for Rover ['*To this day I can't explain that one. I think I liked his Birmingham accent*']. But no clear picture was emerging and therefore the picture of her ideal man forming in my head needed constant readjustment. There were things she praised and condemned within sentences of each another, forcing me into a frantic rewriting of the self I wanted to suggest. At one moment she seemed to be praising emotional vulnerability, and at the next, damning it in favour of independence. Whereas honesty was at one point extolled as the supreme value, adultery was at another justified on account of the greater hypocrisy of marriage.

13. The complexity of her views led to a certain schizophrenia in mine. What sides of myself should I release? How could I avoid alienating her without appearing impossibly bland? While we ate our way through the courses [obstacle courses for young Valmont], I found myself tentatively putting forward one opinion only to subtly alter it a minute later to align it with hers. Every one of Chloe's questions was terrifying, for it might unwittingly contain something that would irrevocably offend her. The main course [the duck for me, the salmon for her] was a marshland sowed with mines – did I think two people should live solely for one another? Had my childhood been difficult? Had I ever been truly in love? What had it been like? Was I an emotional or a cerebral person? Who had I voted for in the last election? What was my favourite colour? Did I think women were more unstable than men?

14. Because it involves the risk of alienating those who do not agree with what one is saying, originality proved wholly beyond me. I merely adjusted myself to whatever I judged Chloe might feel. If she liked tough men, I would be tough, if she liked windsurfing, I would be a windsurfer, if she hated chess, I would hate chess. My idea of what she wanted from a lover could have been compared to a tight-fitting suit and my true self to a fat man, so that the evening was a process resembling a fat man trying to fit into a suit that is too small for him. There was a desperate attempt to repress the bulges that did not fit the cut of the fabric, to shrink my waist and hold my breath so the material would not crack. It was not surprising if my posture was not as spontaneous as I might have liked. How can a fat man in a suit too small for him feel spontaneous? He is so frightened the suit will split, he is forced to sit in complete stillness, holding his breath and praying he can get through the evening without disaster. Love had crippled me.

15. Chloe was facing a different dilemma, for it was time for dessert, and though she had only one choice, she had more than one desire.

'What do you think, the chocolate or the caramel?' she asked [traces of guilt appearing on her forehead]. 'Maybe you can get one and I'll get the other and then we can share.'

I felt like neither, I was not digesting properly, but that was not the point.

'I just love chocolate, don't you?' asked Chloe. 'I can't understand people who don't like chocolate. I was once going out with a guy, this guy Robert I was telling you about, and I was never really comfortable with him, but I couldn't work out why. Then one day it all became clear: he didn't like chocolate. I mean he didn't just not love it, this guy actually hated it. You could have put a bar in front of him and he wouldn't have touched it. That kind of thinking is so far removed from anything I can relate to, you know. Well after that, you can imagine, it was clear we had to break up.'

'In that case we should get both desserts and taste each other's. But which one do you prefer?'

'I don't mind,' lied Chloe.

'Really? Well if you don't mind, then I'll take the chocolate, I just can't resist it. In fact, you see the double chocolate cake at the bottom there? I think I'll order that. It looks far more chocolaty.'

'You're being seriously sinful,' said Chloe, biting her lower lip in a mixture of anticipation and shame, 'but why not? You're absolutely right. Life is short and all that.'

16. Yet again I had lied [I was beginning to hear the sounds of cocks crowing in the kitchen]. I had been more or less allergic to chocolate all my life, but how could I have been honest about my desires in such a situation, where the love of chocolate had been so conclusively identified as an essential criterion of Chloe-compatibility?

17. Nevertheless, my lie was perverse, because of the assumptions it carried about my tastes and habits, namely that they were necessarily less valid than Chloe's and that she would be irretrievably offended by any divergence from her own. I might have made up a moving tale about myself and chocolate ['*I loved it more than anything in the world, but a panel of doctors warned me that I would die if I ate any more of it. I was in therapy for three years thereafter*'] and I might even have received ample sympathy from Chloe – but the risk was simply too high.

18. My lie, as shameful as it was unavoidable, alerted me to a distinction between two kinds of lying, *lying in order to escape* and *lying in order to be loved*. Lies in seduction tend to be very different from lies in other areas. If I lie to the police about the speed at which I am stopped driving, I am doing so for a fairly straightforward motive, in order to escape a fine or an arrest. But lying in order to be loved carries with it the more perverse assumption that *if I do not lie, I cannot be loved*. It is an attitude that sees seductiveness as the emptying of all personal [and hence possibly diverging] characteristics, the true self being judged as irrevocably in conflict with [and hence unworthy of] the perfections found in the beloved.

19. I had lied, but did Chloe like me any the more for it? Was she reaching over to take my hand or suggesting we should skip dessert [though that would perhaps have been asking too much] in order to head home? Certainly not, she merely expressed a certain disappointment, in view of the inferior taste of caramel, that I should have insisted so strongly on taking the chocolate, adding in an offhand way that a choco-phile was in the end perhaps as much of a problem as a choco-phobe.

20. Seduction is a form of acting, a move from spontaneous behaviour towards behaviour shaped by an audience. But just as an actor needs to have a concept of the audience's expec-tations, so too the seducer must have an idea of what the beloved will want to hear – so that if there is a conclusive argument against lying in order to be loved, it is that the actor can have no idea of what his or her audience will be touched by. The only justification for acting would lie in its effectiveness compared with spontaneity, but given the complexity of Chloe's character and doubts as to the attractions of mimetic behaviour, my chances of seducing Chloe could not have been significantly reduced by behaving either honestly or sponta-neously. Inauthenticity seemed only to lead me into farcical somersaults of character and opinion.

21. More often than not, we achieve our goals by coincidence rather than design, dispiriting news for the seducer, who is imbued with the spirit of positivism and rationalism, believ-ing that with enough careful and almost scientific research, laws for the fall into love may be discovered. Seducers proceed in the hope of finding *love hooks* to ensnare the beloved – a certain smile or opinion or way of holding a fork . . . But it is an unfortunate fact that though love hooks exist for everyone, if we hit upon them in the course of seduction, it is more by chance than by calculation. After all, what had Chloe done to make me fall in love with her? My love for her had as much to do with the adorable way she had asked the waiter for some butter as it had with her sharing my views on the merits of Heidegger's *Being and Time*.

22. Love hooks are marked by an extreme idiosyncrasy, apparently defying all logical causal laws. The positive steps I had sometimes seen women make to seduce me had rarely been the ones I had ended up being charmed by. I was prone to falling in love on account of completely tangential or incidental love hooks, ones the seducer had not been sufficiently aware of to push to the fore as valuable assets. I had once fallen in love with a woman who had a slight trace of down on her upper lip. Normally squeamish about this, I had mysteriously been charmed by it in her case, my desire stubbornly deciding to collect there rather than around her warm smile, long blonde hair or intelligent conversation. When I discussed my attraction with friends, I struggled to suggest it had to do with an indefinable 'aura' she possessed – but I could not disguise the fact that I had fallen in love with nothing less than a hairy upper lip. When I saw the woman again, someone must have suggested electrolysis, for the down was gone, and [despite her many qualities] my desire soon followed suit.

23. The Euston Road was still blocked with traffic when we made our way back towards Islington. Long before such questions could have become meaningful, it had been arranged that I would drop Chloe home, but nevertheless the dilemma of the seducer [*To kiss, or not to kiss*] remained

a weighty presence in the car with us. At some point in seduction, the actor must risk losing his audience. The seducing
self may attempt ingratiation by mimetic behaviour, but the
game will eventually require one or other partner to define
the situation, even at the risk of alienating the beloved in the
process. A kiss would change everything, the contact of two
skins would alter our position irrevocably, ending the coded
speech and acknowledging the subtext. However, reaching
the door of 23a Liverpool Road, awed by the dangers of
misreading the signs, I concluded that the moment to propose
a metaphorical cup of coffee had not yet arisen.

24. But after such a tense and chocolate-rich meal, my stom-
ach had suddenly developed quite different priorities, and I
was forced to ask to be allowed up to the flat. I followed
Chloe up the stairs, into the living room and was directed to
the bathroom. Emerging a few minutes later but with my
intentions unaltered, I reached for my coat and announced
to my love, with all the thoughtful authority of a man who
has decided restraint would be best and phantasies entertained
in weeks previous should remain just that, that I had spent a
lovely evening, hoped to see her again soon, and would call
her after the Christmas holidays. Pleased with such a mature
farewell, I kissed her on both cheeks, wished her good-night
and turned to leave the flat.

25. Given the circumstances, it was fortunate that Chloe was
not so easily persuaded, arresting my flight by the ends of
my scarf. She drew me back into the apartment, placed both
arms around me and, looking me firmly in the eye with a
grin she had previously reserved for the idea of chocolate,
whispered, *'We're not children, you know.'*

26. And with these words, she placed her lips on mine and there began the longest and most beautiful kiss mankind has ever known.

On Work and Happiness

The most remarkable feature of the modern workplace has nothing to do with computers, automation or globalization. It lies in the widely-held belief that our work should make us happy. All societies have had work right at their centre; ours is the first to suggest that work could be something other than a punishment or penance. Ours is the first to imply that a sane human being would want to take up work even if he or she wasn't under financial pressure to do so. We are unique too in allowing our choice of work to define who we are, so that the central question we ask of new acquaintances is not where they come from or who their parents are but, rather, what it is they do – as though only this could effectively reveal what gives a human life its distinctive timbre.

It wasn't always like this. Graeco-Roman civilization tended to view work as a chore best left to the slaves. For both Plato and Aristotle, fulfilment could only be reached through the command of a private income which would enable one to escape day-to-day obligations and freely devote oneself to the contemplation of ethical and moral questions. The entrepreneur and merchant played no role in the antique vision of the good life. Early Christianity took a similarly bleak view of labour, adding to the idea that it was a necessary practical burden the even darker thought that man was condemned to toil in order to make up for the sin of Adam. Working conditions, however abusive, could not be improved. Work wasn't accidentally miserable. It was one of the planks upon which earthly suffering was irrevocably founded. St Augustine reminded slaves to obey their masters and accept their pain as part of what he termed, in *The City of God*, the 'wretchedness of man's condition'.

The first signs of the modern, more cheerful attitude to work can be detected in the city states of Italy during the Renaissance and, in particular, in the biographies of the artists of the time. In descriptions of the lives of men like Michelangelo and Leonardo, we find some now familiar-sounding ideas about what our labours could ideally be for us: a path to authenticity and glory. Rather than a burden and punishment, artistic work could allow us to rise above our ordinary limitations. We could express our talents on a page, or on a canvas, in a way we never could in our everyday lives. Of course, this new vision only applied to an artistic elite (no one yet had thought to tell a servant that work could develop his true self: a claim waiting for modern management theory), but it proved to be the model for all successive definitions of happiness earned through work.

It was not until the late eighteenth century that the model was extended far beyond the artistic realm. In the writings of bourgeois thinkers like Benjamin Franklin, Diderot or Rousseau, we see work recategorized not only as a means to earn money, but also as a way of 'becoming oneself'. Here was a reconciliation of necessity and happiness typical of the bourgeois outlook, exactly mirroring the contemporary re-evaluation of marriage. Just as marriage was redescribed as an institution that could deliver both practical benefits and sexual and emotional fulfilment (a handy conjunction once thought impossible by the aristocracy, who saw a need for a mistress and a wife), so too work was alleged to be capable of delivering both the money necessary for survival and the stimulation and self-expression that had once been seen as the exclusive preserve of the leisured.

Simultaneously, people began to experience a new kind of pride in their work, because the way that jobs were handed out took on a semblance of justice. In his *Autobiography*, Thomas Jefferson explained that his proudest achievement had been to create a meritocratic United States, where 'a new aristocracy of virtue and talent' replaced the old aristocracy of unfair privilege and, in many cases, brute stupidity. Meritocracy endowed jobs with a new, quasi-moral quality. Now that prestigious and well-paid posts seemed to be available only on the basis of actual intelligence and ability, your job title could perhaps say something directly meaningful about you. It was no longer possible to argue that professional position was wholly divorced from inner qualities or to claim that the wealthy and powerful must necessarily have attained their positions through corrupt means.

Over the nineteenth century, many Christian thinkers, especially in the United States, changed their views of money accordingly. American Protestant denominations suggested that God required his followers to lead a life that was successful both temporally and spiritually; fortunes in this world were evidence that one deserved a good place in the next – an attitude reflected in the Reverend Thomas P. Hunt's bestseller of 1836, *The Book of Wealth: In Which it is Proved from the Bible that it is the Duty of Every Man to Become Rich*. Wealth came to be described as a reward from God for holiness. John D. Rockefeller was unabashed to state that it was the Lord who had made him rich, while William Lawrence, the Episcopal Bishop of Massachusetts, writing in 1892, argued: 'In the long run, it is only to the man of morality that wealth comes. We, like the Psalmist, occasionally see the wicked prosper, but only occasionally. Godliness is in league with riches.'

In a meritocratic age, demeaning jobs came to seem not

merely regrettable but, just like their more exciting counter-parts, also *deserved*. No wonder people started asking each other what they did – and listening very carefully to the answers.

Though all this seems to offer grounds for celebration, in truth, like attitudes to marriage, modern attitudes to work have unwittingly caused us problems – through their sheer ambition and optimism. Claims are now made on behalf of almost all kinds of work which are patently out of synch with what reality can provide. Some jobs are certainly fulfilling, but the majority are not and never can be. We would there-fore be wise to listen to some of the pessimistic voices of the pre-modern period, if only to stop torturing ourselves for not being as happy in our work as we are told we could be.

William James once made an acute point about the rela-tionship between happiness and expectation. He argued that satisfaction with ourselves does not require us to succeed in every area of endeavour. We are not always humiliated by failing at things, we are only humiliated if we first invest our pride and sense of worth in a given achievement, and then do not reach it. Our goals determine what we will interpret as a triumph and what must count as a failure:

With no attempt there can be no failure and with no failure no humiliation. So our self-esteem in this world depends entirely on what we back ourselves to be and do. It is determined by the ratio of our actualities to our supposed potentialities. Thus:

$$\text{Self-esteem} = \frac{\text{Success}}{\text{Pretensions}}$$

If happiness at work is now so hard to earn, it is because our pretensions have so dramatically outstripped reality. We expect every job to deliver some of the satisfaction available to Freud or Roosevelt. Perhaps we should be reading Marx instead. Of course he was wrong in all his prescriptions for a better world, but he remains rather acute at diagnosing why work is so often miserable. In his *Groundwork of the Metaphysic of Morals* (1785), Immanuel Kant had argued that behaving morally towards other people required that one respect them 'for themselves' instead of using them as a 'means' for one's enrichment or glory. With reference to Kant, in *The Communist Manifesto* (1848), Marx famously accused the bourgeoisie, and its new science, economics, of practising 'immorality' on a grand scale: '[Economics] knows the worker only as a working animal – as a beast reduced to strictest bodily needs.' The wages paid to employees were, said Marx, 'like the oil which is applied to wheels to keep them turning. The true purpose of work is no longer man, but money'.

Marx may have been a poor historian, erratically idealizing the pre-industrial past and unduly castigating the bourgeoisie, but his theories retain a value in capturing and dramatizing an inescapable degree of conflict between employer and employee. Every commercial organization will attempt to gather raw materials, labour and machinery at the lowest possible price to combine them into a product that can be sold at the highest possible price. From the economic perspective, there are no differences between any of the elements in this equation. All are commodities which the rational organization will seek to source cheaply and handle efficiently in the search for profit. And yet, troublingly, there is one difference between 'labour' and other elements which conventional economics does not have a means to represent, or give weight to, but which is nevertheless unavoidably present in the world: the fact that labour feels pain and pleasure. When production lines grow prohibitively expensive, these may be switched off and will not cry at the seeming injustice of their fate. A business can move from using coal to natural gas without the neglected energy source walking off a cliff. But labour has a habit of meeting attempts to reduce its price or presence with emotion. It sobs in toilet cubicles, it drinks to ease its fears of under-achievement and it may choose death over redundancy.

These emotive responses point us to two, perhaps conflicting, imperatives coexisting in the workplace: an economic imperative which dictates that the primary task of business is to realize a profit; and a human imperative which leads employees to hunger for financial security, respect, tenure and even, on a good day, fun. Though the two imperatives may for long periods coexist without apparent friction, what makes anxiety a lingering presence in the lives of all wage-dependent workers is the awareness that, in any serious choice between the two, it is the economic one that must always – by the very logic of the commercial system – prevail. Struggles between labour and capital may no longer, in the developed world at least, be as bare-knuckled as in Marx's day. Yet despite advances in working conditions and employment legislation, workers remain in essence tools in a process in which their own happiness or economic well-being is necessarily incidental. Whatever camaraderie may build up between employer and employed, whatever goodwill workers may display and however many years they may have devoted to a task, they must live with the knowledge and attendant anxiety that their status is not guaranteed – that it remains dependent on both their own performance and the economic well-being of their organizations; that they are hence a means to profit, and never, as they might unshake-ably long for at an emotional level, ends in themselves.

This is all sad, but not half as sad as it is when we blind ourselves to the reality and raise our expectations of our work to extreme levels. A firm belief in the necessary misery of life was for centuries one of mankind's most important assets, a bulwark against bitterness, a defence against dashed hopes – and yet one cruelly undermined by the expectations incu-bated by the modern world-view.

We should perhaps temper our sadness at the end of our holidays by remembering that work is often more bearable when we don't expect it reliably to deliver happiness.

On Going to the Zoo

People look at you strangely if you make a trip to the zoo without a child. You should ideally have a gang of children, evidence of dribbled ice-cream and some balloons as well. Contemplating zoo enclosures with oriental small-clawed otters or leopard geckos hardly seems an adult way to pass the afternoon. The elegant question in London at present is whether you've caught the Ingres show at the National Gallery, not the new pygmy hypo at Regent's Park Zoo.

But my five-year-old nephew pulled out at the last minute (he'd remembered it was his best friend's birthday), and I stubbornly decided to go through with our afternoon as planned. My first thought – after buying an ice-cream, though not a balloon – was how strange animals look. Apart from the odd cat, dog or horse, it's years since I've seen a real animal, an extraordinary, jungle-bookish sort of creature. Take the camel: a u-shaped neck, two furry pyramids, eyelashes that seem coated in mascara, and a set of yellow buckteeth. There was a guide on hand with some facts: camels can go ten days in the desert without drinking; their humps aren't filled with water, it's fat; the eyelashes are designed to keep out sand; and their liver and kidneys extract all moisture from food, leaving their dung dry and compact. They're some of the best-adapted creatures on the planet, concluded the guide – at which point I experienced a childish burst of jealousy at the inadequacy of the human liver and kidney, and our lack of furry bumps to cut out the need for a mid-afternoon snack.

If creatures end up looking so strange, it's a sign of their adaptation to the natural environment, said Darwin, and no one would doubt it in Regent's Park. The Sri Lankan Sloth bear has long mobile lips and two missing upper incisors so that it can suck ants and termites out of their nests, a distinctive facial feature which no one who relied on lunch from a deli would bother with. I had some melancholy thoughts finishing my ice-cream staring at some tar-coloured, pygmy hippos wallowing in mud. The word 'dinosaur' came to mind, not that they resembled them, but they evoked the dinosaur as a byword for fatally slow adaptation to an environment. There are only a few of them left in the world, the future in their natural African habitats lies with lither, more libidinous gazelle-like things.

A zoo visit proves the cliché that it takes all sorts. Every creature seems wonderfully adapted for some things, hopelessly suited for others. The horseshoe crab could never get in the pages of *Vogue* (it looks like a miniature military helmet with bow legs), and couldn't read Gibbon, but it's a star at surviving in deep water and not getting eaten by sharks. It lives quietly, sliding occasionally across the ocean floor to grab a mollusc.

It's hard not to identify with animals, not to land on creatures one might name if forced into an after-dinner round of the what-would-you-be-if-you-had-to-be-an-animal game (sadly losing out to Pictionary as evening entertainment). Flaubert loved the game; in his letters, he compared himself variously to a boa constrictor (1841), an oyster in its shell (1845), and a hedgehog rolling up to protect itself (1853, 1857). I came away identifying with the Malayan tapir, the baby okapi, the llama and the turtle (especially on Sunday evenings).

A zoo unsettles in simultaneously making animals seem

more human and humans more animal. 'Apes are man's closest relative,' reads a caption by the orang-utan enclosure: 'How many similarities can you see?' Far too many for comfort, of course. Shave him, dress him in a T-shirt and tracksuit bottoms, and the one scratching his nose in the corner of the cage is a cousin of mine, except that Jo has a large flat in Belsize Park and spent two weeks in Dorset with his kids this summer. In May 1842, Queen Victoria visited Regent's Park Zoo and, in her diary, noted of a new orang-utan from Calcutta: 'He is wonderful, preparing and drinking his tea, but he is painfully and disagreeably human.' (Reading this, I imagine being captured and placed in a cage like a room in a Holiday Inn, with three meals a day passed through a hatch, and nothing to do other than watch TV – while a crowd of giraffes look on at me, giggling and videoing, licking giant ice-creams, while saying what a short neck I have.)

Inevitably perhaps, I walk out of the zoo with a pair of Desmond Morris spectacles. Calling Sarah up for dinner loses its innocence, it's merely part of the mating ritual of the human species, not fundamentally different from what llamas are up to when they start to whistle strangely at each other on autumn nights.

Then again, there is relief to be found in the ability to view one's antics as complex manifestations of essentially simple animal drives; for food, shelter and survival of one's genetic offspring. I may take out a yearly membership for Regent's Park Zoo.

On Single Men

There are no greater romantics than those who don't have anyone to be romantic with. It is when we are in the depths of loneliness, without the distraction of work or friends, that we are in a position to grasp the nature and necessity of love. It is after a weekend in which the phone has not stirred, in which every meal was prised from a can and consumed in the unconsoling presence of a gravel-voiced BBC narrator – outlining the mating habits of the Kenyan antelope – that we can appreciate why Plato should have declared (*The Symposium*, 416 BC) that a man without love is like a creature with only half its limbs.

Daydreams that arise in such deserted moments could hardly be termed mature, in so far as one associates the word with an awareness of the dangers of idealization and romantic excess. On a train to Edinburgh, I am assigned a seat across from a young woman reading what may be a company report, sucking her way through a carton of apple juice. As we shuttle northwards, I feign a concern for the scenery (parched fields, industrial debris), while remaining glued to the angel. Short brown hair, pale skin, blue-grey eyes, a set of freckles on the nose, a striped sailor top with a small but undeniable splash of what might have been lunch's macaroni. After Manchester, Juliet puts away the company report and takes out a cookbook. *The Food of the Middle East*. Concentration across her brow. Stuffed aubergines. Also, falafel, tabouleh and something that looks like guruko, which requires much spinach. Notes taken in curled, concentrated handwriting.

How little it takes to fall in love. Or at least to fall into the kind of heightened enthusiasm for another person that might be called love, but also crush, sickness or illusion, depending on temperament. By the time the train is past Newcastle, I have thought of marriage, a house in a cherry-tree-lined street, Sunday evenings where she will lay her head beside me and my hand will comb her chestnut strands and we will quietly digest the middle-eastern something-or-other that she made and I will at long last, and for ever more and with infinite gratitude, feel that I have a place in the world.

Such moments punctuate the life of the single male, unfolding without any outward sign, in the presence of faces glimpsed on the Edinburgh train, the lunchtime sandwich line or airport concourse. Pathetic, no doubt, but vital to the institution of the couple. Women should be grateful for the despair of unattached men, for it is the foundation of future loyalty and selflessness – another reason, perhaps, to be suspicious of the romantically successful types, whose charms have left them unacquainted with the tragicomic process of aching for days for a woman they were too shy to address and who stepped off at the next station leaving behind a carton of apple juice and plans for marriage.

On the Charm of Boring Places

1.

The most sincere compliment you could pay Zurich, my home town, is to describe it as one of the great bourgeois cities of the world. This might not, of course, seem like a compliment – the word 'bourgeois' having become for many, since the outset of the Romantic Movement in the early nineteenth century, a significant insult. 'Hatred of the bourgeois is the beginning of wisdom,' felt Gustave Flaubert, a standard utterance for a mid nineteenth-century French writer, for whom such disdain was as much a badge of one's profession as having an affair with an actress and making a trip to the Orient. According to the Romantic value-system, which today still dominates the Western imagination, to be a bourgeois is synonymous with labouring under an obsession with money, safety, tradition, cleaning, family, responsibility, prudishness and (perhaps) bracing walks in the fresh air. Consequently, for about the last two hundred years, few places in the Western world have been quite as deeply unfashionable as the city of Zurich.

2.

Attractive girls born outside Switzerland are particularly against going to Zurich. Such girls prefer LA or Sydney. Even if they are looking for something protestant and homey, they would chose Antwerp or Copenhagen instead.

I've always tried to interest girls in Zurich. I've always thought that a girl who could like Zurich could like important recesses of me. But it's been hard. I recall a trip with Sasha. She was an artist, she was beguiling, she was tricky. We'd have furious arguments, often in the middle of the night. Sometimes the argument went like this:

SHE: You don't like intelligent women, that's why you're disagreeing with me.

HE: I do like intelligent women, but sadly you're not one of them.

Neither of us came out of this sort of thing well. It's a reminder (were one to need it) that lovers practise a form of rudeness that is generally impossible outside of open warfare.

One weekend, Sasha and I flew to Zurich. I tried to point out how exotic Zurich was. Trams were exotic, as was the 'Migros' supermarket, and the light grey concrete of the apartment blocks and the large, solid windows and the veal escalopes. We normally associate the word 'exotic' with camels and pyramids. But perhaps anything different and desirable deserves the word. What I found most exotic was how gloriously boring everything was. No one was being killed by random gunshots, the streets were quiet, everything was tidy and, as everyone says (though you don't see people trying this), it was generally so clean you could eat your lunch off the pavement.

But Sasha was bored. She wanted to go back to Hackney. She couldn't bear the tidiness. On a walk through a park she told me she wanted to graffiti insults on the walls – just to shake the place up a bit. She did a little mock scream, and an old lady looked up from her paper. Her boredom reminded me of my friend Gustave Flaubert, who'd grown up in Rouen, which is perhaps a little bit like Zurich minus the lake. 'I am bored, I am bored, I am bored,' Flaubert wrote in his diary as a young man. He returned repeatedly to the theme of how boring it was to live in France and especially in Rouen. 'Today my boredom was terrible,' he reported at the end of one bad Sunday. 'How beautiful are the provinces and how chic are the comfortably off who live there. Their talk is of taxes and road improvements. The neighbour is a wonderful institution. To be given his full social importance he should always be written in capitals: NEIGHBOUR.' Sasha was bored of Flaubert (she'd tried *A Sentimental Education*, but got bored half way), but she and Flaubert at least agreed on how boring it is to live in a boring place.

However, as mother tends to tell you near the end of the school holidays, it's mostly boring people who get bored – and I began to lose patience with Sasha's boredom. I wanted someone interesting enough inside not to ask of a city that it also be 'interesting'; someone close enough to the well-springs of passion that she wouldn't care if her city wasn't 'fun'; someone sufficiently acquainted with the darker, tragic sides of the human soul to appreciate the stillness of a Zurich weekend. Sasha and I weren't an item for much longer.

3.

But my attraction to Zurich continued. What most appealed to me about Zurich was the image of what was entailed in leading an 'ordinary' life there. To lead an ordinary life in London is generally not an enviable proposition: 'ordinary' hospitals, schools, housing estates or restaurants are nearly always appalling. There are of course great examples, but they are only for the very wealthy. London is not a bourgeois city. It's a city of the rich and the poor.

According to one influential wing of modern secular society, there are few more disreputable fates than to end up being 'like everyone else'; for 'everyone else' is a category that comprises the mediocre and the conformist, the boring and the suburban. The goal of all right-thinking people should be to mark themselves out from the crowd and 'stand out' in whatever way their talents allow. But the desire to be different depends on what it means to be ordinary. There are countries where the communal provision of housing, transport, education or health care is such that citizens will naturally seek to escape involvement with the group and barricade themselves behind high walls. The desire for high status is never stronger than when being ordinary entails leading a life which fails to cater to a median need for dignity and comfort.

Then there are communities, far rarer, many of them imbued with a strong (often Protestant) Christian heritage, where the public realm exudes respect in its principles and architecture, and where the need to escape into a private domain is therefore less intense. Citizens may lose some of their ambitions for personal glory when the public spaces and facilities of a city are themselves glorious to behold. Simply being an ordinary citizen can seem like an adequate destiny. In Switzerland's largest city, the urge to own a car and avoid sharing a bus or train with strangers loses some of the urgency it may have in Los Angeles or London, thanks to Zurich's superlative tram network – clean, safe, warm and edifying in its punctuality and technical prowess. There is little reason to travel alone when, for only a few francs, an efficient, stately tramway will transport one across the city at a level of comfort an emperor would have envied.

4.

There's something faintly embarrassing about loving the Dutch seventeenth-century painter Peter de Hooch deeply, so deeply that one would include him among one's favourite painters of all time. Of the hundred and seventy works assigned to him, most are plain mediocre, overly coarse in the early years or mannered in the later ones. He is operating in a minor genre, his pictures are too pretty and yet not quite pretty enough, not as pretty as a Raphael's or Poussin's, and compared to his countrymen he lacks the inventiveness of Jan Steen, the grace of Vermeer or the density of van Ruïsdael. His morality can appear reactionary, a celebration of the most banal human occupations: delousing, cleaning the patio. He doesn't even paint people very well; look closely at his faces and they are no better than sketches. And yet I've long loved him for reasons very similar to why I love Zurich: because he understands and celebrates bourgeois life, without sentimentalizing it. The world he paints, despite the differences, seems in essence identical to the Zurich I grew up in.

De Hooch is often described as fitting into a tradition of Dutch art and literature which sermonized about the virtues of domesticity. Although de Hooch's paintings do look positively on domestic pursuits, although one would be unlikely to come away from them emboldened to break up one's marriage or leave the kitchen dirty, it seems unfair to label him a crude moralist of domestic virtue. He never tells us that it is important to love one's children or keep the house tidy, he merely provides us with such evocative, moving examples of maternal love and ordered rooms that we would be unlikely to disagree.

Furthermore, his art has none of the smug tone of much overt propaganda of domestic virtue. The simple pleasures of home come across as highly vulnerable achievements. Critics might argue that de Hooch was not painting seventeenth-century Holland the way it really was, they could point out that many women were abused by their husbands, many houses were dirty and primitive, there was a degree of blood and dirt and pain that de Hooch chose not to represent, idealizing matters instead. And yet his art is never sentimental, because it is so infused with an awareness of the darker forces liable at any point to vanquish the hard-won serenity. We don't need to be told that the whole of Holland was not spotlessly clean, we have enough suggestion of it through the many windows at the ends of corridors in de Hooch's canvases. We don't need to be told that the order achieved by women in their homes might be destroyed by war or feckless husbands, we can feel the danger only too well.

In *A Woman with a Young Boy Preparing for School*, a mother butters some bread for her son, he stands dutifully beside her, a little man holding his hat, dressed in a neat grey coat and polished shoes. If the scene is both unsentimental and moving, it is because we are made to feel the evanescence of these intimacies of mother and son. To the left of the canvas, a corridor leads to an open door and out to the street, where there is a large building marked Schole. The boy will soon disguise his debts to his mother who has over the years buttered him loaves and checked his head for lice.

De Hooch's art helps us to recover positive associations of that word with which we may have deeply ambiguous relations: bourgeois. It seems laden with negative connotations, it can suggest conformity, a lack of imagination, stiffness, pedantry and snobbishness. But in de Hooch's world, being bourgeois means dressing in simple but attractive clothes, being neither too vulgar nor too pretentious, having a natural relationship with one's children, recognizing sensual pleasures without yielding to licentiousness. It seems the embodiment of the Aristotelian mean. De Hooch's works perform the valuable task of reminding us of the interest and worth of modest surroundings, quelling vain ambitions and temptations to disengage snobbishly from ordinary routines: the evening meal, the housework, a drink with friends. By paying attention to the beauty of brickwork, of light reflecting off a polished door, of the folds of a woman's dress, de Hooch helps us to find pleasure in these omnipresent but neglected aspects of our world.

5.

Some seventy years before Peter de Hooch painted his greatest works, in a passage in his *Essays*, Michel de Montaigne expressed thoughts that appeared to capture in words some of the atmosphere of de Hooch's art – and, in turn, the qualities upon which the greatness of Zurich is in my view founded. Seeking to remind his readers of the adequacy of ordinary lives, Montaigne wrote:

Storming a breach, conducting an embassy, ruling a nation are glittering deeds. Rebuking, laughing, buying, selling, loving, hating and living together gently and justly with your household – and with yourself – not getting slack nor belying yourself, is something more remarkable, more rare and more difficult. Whatever people may say, such secluded lives sustain in that way duties which are at least as hard and as tense as those of other lives.

Unfortunately, the point keeps getting lost. We keep forgetting that buttering bread for a child and making the bed have their wondrous dimensions. Sir Joshua Reynolds clearly didn't understand. Writing of Jan Steen in the next century, he remarked that though Steen's work was wonderful, 'he would have ranged with the great pillars and supporters of art' had he been able to live in Rome, the greatest city in the world for artists, rather than Leiden, a depressing Zurich-like backwater. In Rome, he would have been inspired to paint really great canvases, he would not have had to limit himself to beggars and merchants, provincial towns and the clutter of daily existence. It is one of the glories of Dutch seventeenth-century art that it proves Sir Joshua Reynolds conclusively wrong. Alongside Steen and Vermeer, Peter de Hooch and his housewives cleaning the patio deserve much of the credit.

6.

Zurich's distinctive lesson to the world lies in its ability to remind us of how truly imaginative and humane it can be to ask of a city that it be nothing other than boring and bourgeois.

On Writing (and Trouts)

I wrote my first book at the age of eight. It was the diary of my summer holiday, spent in the Normandy seaside resort of Houlgate with my parents, dog and sister. 'Yestday nothing much happened. Today the wether is lovely. We went swimming for the hole day. We had salad for lunch. We had a trout for diner. After diner we saw a film about a man that found gold in Peru,' reads a typical entry headed Wendsay 23 of August, 1978 (not dyslexia, just learning English). If the book is unreadable, it's because, despite the best intentions and neat handwriting, the author is unable to capture much of what is actually happening. There is a list of facts, the trout and a weather report, but life has slipped out of the picture. It's like watching a home video, in which you're shown only the feet or the clouds, and wonder, bemused, what might be going on at head-level.

Much writing is like that. Even when the spelling improves, it takes a struggle to arrange words so they do justice to our intentions. Typically, the written account grazes the surface of an event, we see a sunset and later in the diary, fumble for something and call it 'beautiful' when we know it was a lot more, but the more can't be fixed and is soon forgotten. We want to capture what happened today, and so draw up a list of where we went and what we saw, but leave the page knowing that there were evanescent things that we have failed to describe, but which we suspect may hold the key to the reality of the day.

It takes more to capture life than a faithful record of sense-experience. The data of what we see does not make art: it is only when a process of selection, choice and thought have been applied that things stand a chance of looking natural. Here is Virginia Woolf telling her diary what happened to her on 15 February 1915:

Leonard [the husband] and I both went up to London this afternoon; L. to the Library, & I to ramble about the West End, picking up clothes. I am really in rags. With age one's less afraid of superb shops. I swept about in Debenham's & Marshalls. Then I had tea & rambled down to Charing Cross in the dark, making up phrases & incidents to write about. Which is, I expect, the way one gets killed. I bought a ten & elevenpenny blue dress, in which I sit at this moment.

It's hard to say exactly why this works, why the life has not drained out of the account. Woolf just seems to have picked on the right details, she has known where to look; something in the confession about superb shops, in the ability to recognize eccentricities on Charing Cross Road, the intimate 'in which I sit at this moment . . .'

A paradox of other people's books is that they often tell us more about our own life than we have been able to grasp alone. It is the words on someone else's page that return us to a more vivid sense of who we are, and what our world is like. It is, for instance, Goethe's Young Werther who teaches me what it means to be young and unrequited in love, it is Flaubert's Homais who I see in the learned idiocy of the politician or adman, it is because of those painful passages in Proust that I can gain some understanding of what's going on when I'm destroyed by jealousy.

But the value of great books is not limited to depiction of emotions and people akin to those in our own life; it stretches to an ability to describe these *far better* than we would have been able, to put a finger on perceptions that we both recognize *as our own*, but could not have formulated *on our own*.

We might, for instance, have known someone like Proust's fictional Duchesse de Guermantes. We might have felt there was something superior and insolent in this woman's manner, without knowing quite what, until Proust discreetly points out in brackets how the Duchesse reacts when, during a smart dinner, a Mme de Gallardon makes the error of being a little overfamiliar with the Duchesse, known also as Oriane des Laumes, and addresses her by her first name.

'Oriane' (at once Mme des Laumes looked with amused astonishment towards an invisible third person, whom she seemed to call to witness that she had never authorized Mme de Gallardon to use her Christian name) . . .

An effect of reading a book which has devoted attention to noticing such faint yet vital tremors is that, once we've put the volume down and resumed our own life, we may attend to precisely the things which the author would have responded to had he or she been in our company. Our mind will be like a radar newly attuned to pick up certain objects floating through consciousness, the effect will be like bringing a radio into a room that we had thought silent, and realizing that the silence only existed at a particular frequency and that all along we in fact shared the room with waves of sound coming in from a Ukranian station or the night-time chatter of a minicab firm. Our attention will be drawn to the shades of the sky, to the changeability of a face, to the hypocrisy of a friend, or to a submerged sadness about a situation which we had previously not even known we could feel sad about.

On Comedy

1.

The summer of 1831 found King Louis-Philippe of France in a confident mood. The political and economic chaos of the July Revolution, which had brought him to power the year before, was giving way to prosperity and order. He had in place a competent team of officials led by his prime minister, Casimir Périer; he had travelled around the northern and eastern parts of his realm and been given a hero's welcome by the provincial middle classes. He lived in splendour in the Palais-Royal in Paris; banquets were thrown in his honour every week; he loved eating (especially foie gras and game); he had a vast personal fortune and a loving wife and children.

But there was one thing to cloud Louis-Philippe's composure. In late 1830, a twenty-eight-year-old unknown artist by the name of Charles Philipon had launched a satirical magazine, *La Caricature*, in which he had represented the head of the king, whom he accused of corruption and incompetence on a grand scale, in the shape of a pear. Not only did Philipon's cartoons allude unkindly to the king's swollen cheeks and bulbous forehead, the French word *poire*, meaning fathead or mug, neatly indicated a less than respectful attitude towards Louis-Philippe's powers of administration.

The king was enraged. He instructed his agents to obstruct the magazine's production and buy up all copies from Parisian kiosks. When this failed to deter Philipon, in November 1831 the caricaturist was charged with having 'caused offence to the person of the king' and ordered to appear in court in Paris. Speaking before a packed chamber, Philipon thanked the prosecutors for arresting a dangerous man like himself, but pointed out that the government had been negligent in their pursuit of the king's detractors. It should be a priority to try to arrest anything in the shape of a pear, even pears themselves should be locked up. There were thousands of them on trees all over France, every one of these fruits a criminal fit for incarceration, mocked Philipon. The court was not amused. He was sent to prison for six months, and when he repeated the pear joke in a new magazine, *Le Charivari*, the following year, he was put straight back in jail – spending, in all, two years behind bars for drawing the monarch as a piece of fruit.

2.

Louis-Philippe would not have responded in such a way if humour were just a game. As he was the first to recognize, jokes are a way of anchoring a criticism. They are another way of complaining: about arrogance, cruelty or pomposity, about departures from virtue and good sense.

If they are a particularly effective way of complaining, it is because they communicate a lesson while seeming only to entertain us. Comics have no need to deliver a sermon outlining abuses of power. They lead us to acknowledge in a chuckle the aptness of their complaints against authority.

Furthermore (the prison experiences of Philipon notwithstanding), the apparent innocence of jokes allows comics to convey messages that could be dangerous or impossible to voice directly. Historically, it is the jesters at court who have been allowed to tell royals serious things that could not have been said to them seriously (when King James I of England, who presided over a notoriously corrupt clergy, had trouble fattening up one of his horses, Archibald Armstrong, the court fool, was said to have told him that he had only to make the horse into a bishop for the creature rapidly to put on the necessary pounds).

That said, not every exalted person is ripe for comic treatment. We rarely laugh at a doctor performing an important surgical operation. Yet we may laugh at a doctor who, after an operation, returns home and intimidates his wife and daughters by talking to them in pompous medical jargon. We laugh at what is excessive and disproportionate. We laugh at kings whose self-image has outgrown their worth, whose goodness has not kept up with their power. We laugh at high-status individuals who have forgotten their humanity and are abusing their privileges. We laugh at, and through our laughter criticize, evidence of injustice and excess.

In the hands of the best comics, laughter hence acquires a moral purpose, jokes become attempts to cajole others into reforming their characters and habits. Jokes are a way of sketching a political ideal, of creating a more equitable and saner world. Wherever there is injustice or delusion, space opens up for humour-clad criticisms. As Samuel Johnson saw it, satire is only another way, and a particularly effective one, of 'censuring wickedness or folly'. In the words of John Dryden, 'the true end of satire is the amendment of vices'.

3.

Not only is humour a useful tool with which to attack high-status others, it may also help us to make sense of, and moderate, our own status anxieties.

Much that we find funny focuses on situations or feelings that, in ordinary life, we would be liable to encounter with embarrassment or shame. The greatest comics place their fingers on vulnerabilities that we cannot examine in the light of day; they pull us from our lonely relationship with our most awkward sides. The more private and intense the worry, the greater the possibility of laughter, laughter being a tribute to the skill with which the unmentionable has been skewered.

Unsurprisingly therefore, much humour reveals an attempt to name, and thereby contain, anxiety about status. It reassures us that there are others in the world no less envious or socially fragile than we are; that there are fellow spirits waking up in the early hours tormented by their financial performance; and that beneath the sober appearance society demands of us, most of us are going a little out of our minds – giving us cause to hold out a hand to our comparably tortured neighbours.

Rather than *mocking* us for our concern with status, the kindest comics *tease* us: they criticize us while implying that we remain essentially acceptable. Thanks to their skills, we acknowledge with an open-hearted laugh bitter truths about ourselves that we might have recoiled from in anger or hurt had they been levelled at us in an ordinary, accusatory way.

4.

Comics, no less than other artists, hence slip rewardingly into Matthew Arnold's definition of art as a discipline offering criticism of life. Their work strives to amend both the injustices of power and the excesses of our envy towards those higher in the social system. Like tragedies, they are motivated by some of what is most regrettable about our condition.

The underlying, unconscious aim of comics may be to bring about – through the adroit use of humour – a world in which there will be a few less things to laugh about.

POCKET PENGUINS

36. **Muriel Spark** The Snobs
37. **Steven Pinker** Hotheads
38. **Tony Harrison** Under the Clock
39. **John Updike** Three Trips
40. **Will Self** Design Faults in the Volvo 760 Turbo
41. **H. G. Wells** The Country of the Blind
42. **Noam Chomsky** Doctrines and Visions
43. **Jamie Oliver** Something for the Weekend
44. **Virginia Woolf** Street Haunting
45. **Zadie Smith** Martha and Hanwell
46. **John Mortimer** The Scales of Justice
47. **F. Scott Fitzgerald** The Diamond as Big as the Ritz
48. **Roger McGough** The State of Poetry
49. **Ian Kershaw** Death in the Bunker
50. **Gabriel García Márquez** Seventeen Poisoned Englishmen
51. **Steven Runciman** The Assault on Jerusalem
52. **Sue Townsend** The Queen in Hell Close
53. **Primo Levi** Iron Potassium Nickel
54. **Alistair Cooke** Letters from Four Seasons
55. **William Boyd** Protobiography
56. **Robert Graves** Caligula
57. **Melissa Bank** The Worst Thing a Suburban Girl Could Imagine
58. **Truman Capote** My Side of the Matter
59. **David Lodge** Scenes of Academic Life
60. **Anton Chekhov** The Kiss
61. **Claire Tomalin** Young Bysshe
62. **David Cannadine** The Aristocratic Adventurer
63. **P. G. Wodehouse** Jeeves and the Impending Doom
64. **Franz Kafka** The Great Wall of China
65. **Dave Eggers** Short Short Stories
66. **Evelyn Waugh** The Coronation of Haile Selassie
67. **Pat Barker** War Talk
68. **Jonathan Coe** 9th & 13th
69. **John Steinbeck** Murder
70. **Alain de Botton** On Seeing and Noticing